Margaret Burgess.

ST. HILDA
AND HER TIMES

SYLVIA MUNDAHL-HARRIS

GW00771258

ISBN 0 905355 18 0

© Abbey Press, 1985.

Printed and Published by Abbey Press (Whitby).
4/5 Grape Lane, Whitby, Yorkshire.

ST. HILDA. Imaginative representations of St. Hilda show her holding the church of her patronage. Here she holds the chapel of St. Hilda's School, Whitby, the place where this finely carved and inspiring statue stands. (By kind permission of the Rev. Mother O.H.P.) ...

CANONISATION

St. Hilda herself, like most of the early saints, was never officially canonised as a saint by the Roman church as the ritual was not introduced until much later.

SAINT HILDA AND HER TIMES

Every visitor to Whitby sees the ruins of the great abbey of St. Peter and St. Hilda dominating the East Cliff and many climb the 199 well-worn steps to look at the ruins more closely.

How and when did the abbey come there and who was Saint Hilda?

Hilda lived in the 7th century A.D. It takes some mental effort and imagination, as well as knowing something of history, to get back to those days and circumstances. The ruined abbey seen today was built nearly five hundred years after Hilda's time but the strength of her personality and character still pervades the place.

Saint Hilda,—or Hild, to give her the correct Anglo-Saxon name, which means "battle"—was born in 614 A.D. into the royal house of Northumbria.

Northumbria meant what it said, the land north of the Humber. It was sub-divided into two kingdoms, Bernicia in the north with its centre at Bamburgh, and Deira in the south, probably centred near Catterick.

The "Kings" were little more than tribal warrior chiefs, fighting against neighbouring kingdoms and often feuding with their own families. Indeed, they were expected to die in battle. Their history is largely one of succeeding to their kingdoms, fighting battles and being slain.

EARLY YEARS

614

Hilda was a great niece of Edwin, the king of Northumbria at the time of her birth. She was the second daughter of Hereric (Edwin's nephew) and Breguswith, of whom we know little. Hereric was apparently exiled and living under the protection of the British (as opposed to Anglo-Saxon) King Cerdic of Elmet, a small kingdom near what is now Leeds.

Breguswith, Hilda's mother, had a prophetic dream in which she found Hereric had been taken away and although she searched everywhere she could find no trace of him. In the search she found a most precious jewel hidden in her garments and it gave off such a brilliant light that the whole land was lit by it. Hilda was said to be the fulfilment of this dream.

Soon afterwards Hereric was murdered by poisoning, though we must remember that at the time death from violent internal pain was always put down to poisoning. However his death was brought about, Hilda and her elder sister Hereswith were left fatherless to be brought up by their mother. It is obvious that Hilda would be strongly influenced by female company and management in her youth, which would stand her in good stead when she later ran her own monastery.

It would appear that in her early years she was brought up in a pagan household. About the pagan religion and practices little is known except that they had temples and sacred places where idols were worshipped, sacrifices offered and various rituals performed, especially those connected with magic, black and white.

CHRISTIANITY
625

There had been many converts to Christianity in England after Pope Gregory I had sent Augustine to Canterbury to found a mission in 597 A.D. Edwin, king of Northumbria was not one of the converts, but continued to practise his own pagan rites. Edwin married as his second wife, Ethelburga, daughter of the king of Kent. The marriage was sanctioned only on his giving a pledge that his wife,—who had already been baptised by the Pope's representative in Kent, Paulinus— should be free to practise the Christian religion.

Edwin further promised that he would be willing to become a Christian if: "on examination his advisors decided that it appeared more holy and acceptable to God than their own pagan religion." (Bede).

In 625 Paulinus, now a bishop, came with the betrothed Ethelburga from Kent to Northumbria as her chaplain. Hilda would then be a child of eleven, living at Edwin's court.

It was two years before Edwin accepted the Christian faith, despite the urgings of Paulinus and letters from the Pope in Rome. Then it was only an attempt to assassinate him with a poisoned dagger,—an attempt from which he was saved when one of his noblemen, Lilla, threw himself in front of the king and was slain instead. (Lilla's name is perpetuated in a moorland cross near Whitby).

Edwin then said that he would serve Christ, but he would actually be baptised only if Christ sent victory over his enemies. He did, however, permit his infant daughter Eanfrid to be baptised by Paulinus with twelve members of his wife's family.

Hilda must have known all this and have heard and been moved by the preaching of Paulinus. We even have a description of what he looked like: "A tall man having a slight stoop with thick black hair and an ascetic face and a thin, hooked nose; and a venerable and majectic presence." (Bede). He was the first great Christian bishop and evangelist with whom Hilda came in contact.

BAPTISM

After recovering from the wound received at the attempted assassination, Edwin went off to settle the score with the south Saxon king, and returning victorious decided to fulfil his vow and be baptised.

Firstly he held a long discussion with his elders and pagan priests and they seemed to have accepted that the Christian was the stronger religion which could confer more benefits. One of these priests drew the well known analogy of the sparrow.

"When we compare the present life of man with that time of which we have no knowledge," he said, "it seems to me like the swift flight of a lone sparrow through the banqueting hall where you sit in the winter months to dine with your thanes and counsellors. The sparrow flies in through one door of the hall and out through another".

"While he is inside he is safe from the winter storms, but after a few moments of comfort he vanishes into the darkness from whence he came. Similarly, man appears on earth for a little while, but we know nothing of what went before this life, and what follows. Therefore, if this new teaching can reveal any more certain knowledge, it seems only right that we should follow it."

4

The king took the priests' advice and gave orders to have the pagan temples destroyed and the idols broken. Then, at York, Edwin had a special little church built of timber and there he and all his followers were baptised.

Among them was Hilda, for when a king was converted all his subjects were expected to follow suit. Liberty of conscience would not have been permitted. Not that the young Hilda would have wanted to stay a pagan.

We can imagine the effect on a thirteen-year-old girl of witnessing the stately procession at the mass baptism in the river Ouse. Baptism was a very serious step to take and was one of the most important rituals in the church of that time. Not only was it the sign of becoming a Christian and entering the church (early churches forbade any but the baptised to enter their sacred building) it was also a visible act of washing away all pagan error before entering the new life.

The temporary church was near enough to the river for the purpose of baptism and the ceremony would afterwards be continued within it. On its site Edwin later built "a noble stone basilica". (There were plenty of noble Roman stones lying about in York!)

Edwin made Paulinus Bishop of York and from then on the city became an important church centre, as Pope Gregory had hoped it would be.

THE ROYAL HOUSEHOLD

Until Hilda was nineteen she presumably lived at the court of King Edwin, who was claimed to be the first "King of all the English." He controlled all the land north of the Humber and southern Scotland as well as being overlord of East Anglia and recognised even in Kent. We know of two royal capitals, Yeavering in north Northumberland and Catterick in Yorkshire. Probably Hilda had spent time at both these places as well as Bamburgh, the ancient stronghold of the Northumbrian kings.

Life at court was probably comfortable and the people well provided for by the standards of the time. It had been said that there was such peace in the land that a woman with a newborn babe could safely cross from coast to coast without being molested. Edwin had bronze cups put by springs so that all might drink, and no one stole them.

The recent discovery of a buried ship and kingly treasure at Sutton Hoo, which are from this period, show the luxuries and beautiful things which people of royal houses could acquire. There were delicately made gold ornaments and brooches, cups and spoons and bowls made of silver, armour and weapons decorated with precious stones, indeed, one belt was inset with four-thousand cut garnets. They show not nearly as low a standard of living as one might imagine in barbarous times.

During this time Hilda's sister was married to just such a king of East Anglia. We have no record of any suggested husband for Hilda. At that time, being a widow or even renouncing one's husband would not be a barrier to entering a nunnery. The test was that one should be celibate from then on.

We do know that when Hilda was nineteen disaster struck and there was an end to the fifteen years of comparative peace and pleasant life in the royal household.

HOLY ISLAND

In 632 Penda of Mercia, a member of the Mercian royal house but not yet king, allied with Cadwalla—the "British" king of Gwynedd—and invaded Northumbria.

Mercia was the kingdom to the south-west of Northumbria, which today is the midlands. Cadwalla controlled much of Wales and was a long-term enemy of Edwin, accusing him of slaughtering a large band of Welsh monks sent out to seek peace.

At a battle at Hatfield Chase Edwin and his eldest son were killed and their army routed. His second son surrendered and was murdered at Penda's court.

What happened to the women?

We know that the Christian bishop, Paulinus, took Queen Ethelburga back to her homeland in Kent. The small children were sent to a relative in France, where they died young. Only a daughter, Eanfleda, survived.

Did Hilda go with Ethelburga or did she retreat to the royal stronghold at Bamburgh, which still held out?

As Penda carried out deliberate devastation of Northumbria with fire and sword it fell into its two ancient kingdoms of Bernicia and Deira. Cadwalla burnt the royal centre at Yeavering and it never recovered.

The descendants of the ancient kings of Bernicia had been exiled as children to Iona, where they had been brought up by the Celtic monks on that island. They now returned to Bamburgh. The eldest was killed fighting against Cadwalla, but his brothers Oswald and Oswy were destined to become kings of Northumbria.

A year after returning, Oswald defeated and killed Cadwalla at the battle of Heavenfield near Hadrian's Wall at Hexham. Before the battle Oswald, who was a devout Christian, set up a wooden cross with his own hands. In later years splinters of wood from this cross were said to have miraculous healing powers. Every year monks from the monastery at Hexham made a pilgrimage to the spot on the anniversary of the battle.

Oswald then ruled Northumbria for nine years. Immediately following his victory he sent to Iona asking for a missionary bishop and Aidan was sent.

Oswald offered him land on which to found a monastery and Aidan chose Lindisfarne,—Holy Island. It was sufficiently remote and secure to carry on the monastic life of prayer and study and yet accessible at low tide so that missionaries could go out on to the mainland.

Aidan set up a community of monks who went out to convert and teach. They lived in great austerity and simplicity, their buildings being of timber with turf or reed thatching. Nevertheless their influence throughout Northumbria was very great and there is no doubt that Hilda was much influenced by

Aidan, not only by his teaching but also his rejection of worldly goods. All gifts that he received he promptly gave away to the poor and the starving,—of whom there were many, after the devastating wars.

Hilda seems to have spent the next twelve years in Northumbria, probably engaged in charitable work amongst the poor and sick. We are told:

She spent 33 years most nobly in secular occupation and then dedicated the remainder of her life even more nobly to our Lord in the monastic life.

TROUBLED TIMES

642

Throughout his reign Oswald had trouble from Penda, the pagan who had killed Edwin and was now king of Mercia. It was a struggle for military supremacy, for conquest of territory and possession of the enemy's goods rather than a battle between Christianity and paganism as Bede would have us believe.

In one of these struggles in 642 Oswald was killed at Maserfelth (probably Oswestry in Shropshire). His body was hacked to pieces by his enemies. His arm and hand,—which had given generously to the poor and needy and to the church— were preserved in a silver casket at Bamburgh, the place where Hilda probably was. His head was buried at Lindisfarne—which he had been instrumental in founding—and the rest of his bones went eventually to Bardney Abbey in Lincolnshire.

Oswald was regarded as a Christian martyr and he quickly became a saint. Many miracles are said to have taken place through contact with his relics.

As a result of his defeat terrible times came once again to Northumbria. Oswy succeeded his brother Oswald, but he controlled only the north, Bernicia. Control of Deira passed to a relative, King Oswin, reputed to be a man of great holiness and piety who ruled for seven years. It is of him the famous story of St. Aidan and the horse is told.

Oswin gave him a very fine horse. Aidan promptly gave it to a destitute beggar. Oswin was not best pleased saying that if he must give a horse away he could have given a less valuable one. To which Aidan replied:

"Your Majesty, is this foal of a mare more valuable to you than this child of God?"

Oswin brooded a while and then humbly acknowledged that Aidan was right.

They were troubled times indeed; for Aidan, who was based at Lindisfarne and had great influence over St. Hilda—favoured Oswin of south Northumbria rather than Oswy whose centre was so near to him at Bamburgh.

Nevertheless, when Penda beseiged Bamburgh and tried to set fire to it, it was Aidan who prayed and changed the wind.

WEARMOUTH

In order to gain control of all Northumbria, Oswy determined to make war against his kinsman Oswin. Near Catterick, Oswin decided to disband inferior forces and discuss terms of settlement with Oswy. He was staying in the house of an earl whom he considered his best friend, but the earl betrayed him and Oswy had him foully murdered and himself assumed kingship of the whole of Northumbria.

Four years before that, Hilda, inspired by Aidan's teaching, had decided to become a nun and had left for East Anglia, from where she would take a ship to join her widowed sister, Hereswith, who was already at a convent at Chelles in northern France. Hilda's nephew, Adwulf, was king of the East Angles at that time. Bede tells us that the daughters of noble families were often sent to Chelles for their education,—an early example of the distant boarding school!

Before leaving Northumbria she had renounced her home and all that she possessed. Hilda stayed at her nephew's court for a whole year making her preparations for departure, when she was urged by Aidan to return to Northumbria where he would have a piece of land, one hide, bestowed on her to found a monastery with a few devout companions.

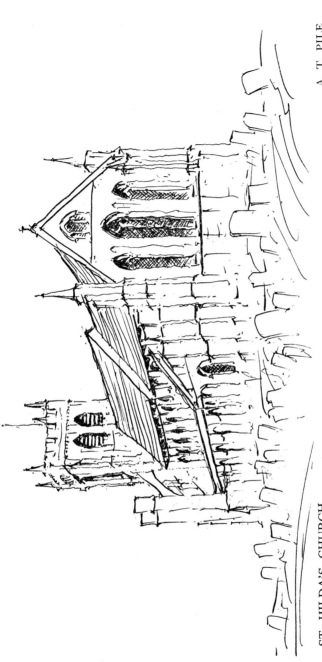

ST. HILDA'S CHURCH

HARTLEPOOL. The graceful and very beautiful Abbey Church of St. Hilda testifies to the continuing Christian faith maintained here since her time. It was dedicated to St. Hilda in the thirteenth century. It is probable that her monastery stood on the same site or very close to it.

A. T. PILE

LILLA CROSS.   The stone sentinel named
(perhaps by Hilda) after the gallant warrior who
saved Edwin's life stands on the lonely moor
and marks the safe track between Whitby and
Hackness. (Reproduced by kind permission of
  Whitby Literary and Philosophical Society).

A "hide" was an indefinite measure, said to be enough to support one household and estimated now to be perhaps 120 acres.

The site of the Lady Hilda's first monastery was on the north bank of the river Wear,—dominated today by the industrial town of Sunderland. The exact spot is not known but it is more than likely that it was very near to the monastery founded some thirty years later by Benedict Biscop, part of whose church still stands.

So completely has Monkwearmouth changed, with its heavy traffic, its tangle of cranes towering over the warehouses and dockyards, that it takes an immense effort of imagination to picture the rather bleak, windswept river mouth that the Lady Hilda knew.

HARTLEPOOL

649

Hilda stayed in Monkwearmouth only a short while and then in 649 Aidan appointed her Abbess of Hartlepool. In that time it was called "Heretu" which means the place of the Hart. Deer would be plentiful in the heavily wooded area.

Hartlepool itself, where the monastery was, jutted out into the north sea much as Holy Island does and must have reminded Lady Hilda very forcibly of that place. To the south the wide Tees estuary flooded out into extensive marshes, with no landing places anywhere. Hartlepool, however, stands firmly on rock.

The monastery had been founded by a certain lady Heiu (or Hegu) sent by Aidan. She is said to have been "the first woman in the kingdom of Northumbria to take vows and be clothed as a nun". So it appears that Aidan was the first to recognise and support the equality of women in the religious life.

It is plain that these monasteries were for communities of men and women who had taken vows of poverty, chastity and obedience. It seems that monks retained the right to travel about the countryside whilst nuns, once professed, remained in their monasteries.

It appears that Heiu had gone to Tadcaster, perhaps preferring to live under King Oswin's rule in the south rather than in Oswy's land with the constant threat of Penda's attacks.

Bede says of Hilda at this time:

Bishop Aidan and other devout men who knew her and admired her innate wisdom and love of God often used to visit and advise her.

Bishop Aidan did not live to see Lady Hilda at Whitby, for he died in 651, while she was still at Hartlepool.

WHITBY

More settled times were coming, for in 655 Oswy won a great victory over the Mercian pagan king Penda who had previously slain in battle Edwin and Oswald, Oswy's brother. The battle was in South Yorkshire at a place called Winwaed. We know it was beside a river which was in flood and more of the enemies were drowned than those killed in battle.

Lady Hilda's fortunes were directly affected by the victory, for before the battle Oswy made a vow that if victory were granted he would give his infant daughter Aelfleda in perpetual virginity to the church. Although only a year old, the little girl was given to Hilda at Hartlepool to be brought up and dedicated to the church.

Oswy also promised to give twelve grants of land to set up monasteries—six in north Northumbria and six in the south. This too affected Hilda, for she received a grant of ten hides of land to form a monastery at Streonshalh (the Anglo-Saxon name for Whitby.) She therefore had about 1200 acres around Whitby.

Streonshalh is said to mean the haven of Streon, but Bede calls it the haven of the watch tower, which would confirm the theory that the Romans had a signal station there (as well as at Goldsborough, five miles north of Whitby) until the early fifth century. Roman coins have been found there.

When Lady Hilda came it was a very exposed and wind-whipped site high on the east cliff which she chose to establish her community of men and women. The rough sea swirled on the rocks at the base of the cliffs and the waves drove far up the river, unhindered by the sheltering piers which exist today.

The west cliff was very difficult of access, as it was all marshland at the base. The only ford was beside Spital Bridge and went across to what we now call Bog Hall. The mouth of the River Esk was, in effect, a wide marshy estuary.

The first available landing spot must have been well up the River Esk, perhaps about where the shipyard is today. It is even possible that the very first settlement was in this little valley beside Spital Beck, where baptisms could easily take place in the river, baptism being one of the most important rites of the church,—a veritable washing away of paganism.

No doubt the first buildings were of timber and thatch, and stone would replace these as the monastery expanded. After shelters for the community the building of the church would be next. Probably these simple structures were put up before the final move from Hartlepool took place, for there was, after all a two year gap between little Aelfleda's arrival and the exodus to Whitby.

There would have to be a water supply and digging wells was hard work. Perhaps the well from the Roman signal station was still there.

Many early monasteries deliberately chose isolated and desolate sites for privacy and security. As we climb the broad steps of the 199 church stairs we remember that Lady Hilda's monks and nuns had to make their way up a rough and steep stony track to reach the monastery from the riverside.

Originally there were possibly twelve monks and the same number of nuns, but numbers increased rapidly. Priests were needed to conduct the services and strong men to do the heavy building work. Slaves were still used, but not by monasteries. (Aidan, for example, used money given to him to buy slaves their freedom).

It was an immense undertaking, but nevertheless, Bede writes:

Hilda carried out her appointed task with great energy. She established the same regular life as in her former monastery and taught the observance of righteousness, mercy, purity and other virtues, but especially in peace and charity.

We must remember all the years of war, looting, greed and barbarism that Hilda had witnessed and turned away from.

After the example of the primitive church, no one there was rich or poor, for everything was held in common and none possessed any personal property. So great was her prudence that not only ordinary folk, but kings and princes used to come and ask her advice in their difficulties.

There can be no doubt that Lady Hilda worked with great energy, for from absolutely nothing in 657 she built up such a thriving, well established community that seven years later a meeting of all the chief leaders in the church, summoned by King Oswy himself, took place there,—the famous Synod of Whitby, (although at that date it is wrong to call it Whitby, which is a Danish name).

Whitby had developed quickly as a centre of learning and training for the priesthood. Bede tells us that no fewer than five men who became bishops were trained there, at least one of whom, Oftfor, was with Hilda at Hartlepool; he later went to Kent to study under Archbishop Theodore and then made his way to Rome and back to England, which was a long and terrible journey at that time. Another of Hilda's pupils was St. John of Beverley.

THE CELTIC QUESTION

The division and arguments between the English Christians, converted from Rome, and the Celtic (British) Christians went back into history.

Before the coming of the Angles and Saxons from north-west Europe many romanised Britons had been converted to Christianity. They then had to retreat before the invaders. They went to Wales and Cornwall and across the sea to Ireland, Brittany and even as far as the Basque region of Spain. They were the Celts, who even to this day retain their desire for a separate identity.

Many religious communities were founded in Ireland. In the fifth century we have St. Patrick there, and St. David in Wales and Cornwall. In the sixth century St. Columba left Ireland to found a mission to Scotland on the island of Iona. The brothers in the monastery which he founded were not only to lead a life of self-denial and austerity, they were also to study the scriptures and go out on missions.

From Iona abbeys were founded at Melrose and Dunkeld and in 634 at Lindisfarne by Bishop Aidan. The kings Oswald and Oswy were brought up as boys on Iona. Thus the Celtic church had a very strong hold on the north of England, but in the south it was different.

In 597 Augustine had been sent from Rome by Pope Gregory I to convert the English. Canterbury became the centre of the mission and kept in as close touch with Rome as possible. It was by no means easy, for the journey was long and fraught with danger, but somehow they managed.

As we saw, Hilda herself was baptised and taught by Paulinus from Canterbury, but she was also greatly influenced by Bishop Aidan from Iona.

EASTER

The inevitable conflict came to a head over the question of the exact time at which Easter should be celebrated.

King Oswy kept to the Celtic custom, which meant that he celebrated Easter while his wife Queen Eanfleda followed the Roman custom and was keeping the Lenten fast and celebrating Palm Sunday.

So the synod was called at Whitby to decide the question once and for all. It all seems complicated and a bit unnecessary to us, until we remember that until Pope Gregory's time the months were lunar, a difficulty which had to be overcome by inserting an extra month (ie: thirteen 28-day months in a year). Even so it was difficult to reconcile the seasons with the dates.

It was known that Christ was crucified just after the Jewish Passover and the Jews had their own way of working out when this occurred. Easter Sunday should therefore be the day after that Jewish sabbath (Saturday). Christian bishops in Rome had spent much time working out when that should be but the Celtic church had continued to use its own method of calculation.

WILFRED

One after another, the company assembled for the great Synod. Some came on horseback and some by boat. The royal party arrived with Oswy and his son Alchfrid, the patron of Wilfred. Wilfred came with the chief representative of the Roman Church, Agilbert, bishop of the West Saxons (Hampshire and Dorset area), a priest named Agatho, later to become Pope, and James, a pupil of Paulinus.

To support Lady Hilda and her community in the Celtic view Bishop Coleman had sailed from the northerly Lindisfarne. The two brothers, Chad and Cedd, who had trained there and were now bishops, came. Cedd was the founder and abbot of Lastingham, not far from Whitby. He acted as interpreter as he spoke Latin, English and Celtic. Chad had been in Ireland and was to become Bishop of Mercia with his see at Lichfield.

Bishop Wilfred (not to be confused with the other bishop of the same name who trained at Whitby) had received his early training with Bishop Aidan. When he was about eighteen he went to Rome and was deeply impressed by all that he saw in the old imperial city and by the majesty and power of the church with the Bishop of Rome, the Pope, as its head.

When he compared this with the humble, struggling and poverty stricken church in England, Wilfred determined that things must change. On his return journey he stayed almost two years in Gaul (France) where he continued his studies, decided to become a monk, and received the tonsure from the Archbishop of Paris.

THE TONSURE

The hair was shaved in the middle of the head, so that the surrounding hair might be a symbol of the crown of thorns. The disputes about the form of the monk's tonsure may seem trivial to us, but it was of great importance at the time as the Celtic monks shaved the hair at the front of the head, from ear to ear, in order to stress their Celtic rather than English origin; the Druid priests had done likewise.

This was one of the questions to be settled at the Synod of Whitby.

Wilfred seems to have been very clever and learned, but with a tendency to believe,—like Napoleon—that God is on the side of the big battalions; which in this instance was the wealth and power of the Roman church. He did not seek wealth for himself, though much was given to him, but rather that it could be used to extend the power and glory of the church. He became a great friend of Alchfrid the ruler of Deira. He gave Wilfred a monastery and forty hides of land at Ripon, turning out some Scottish monks who were there so that Wilfred could become abbot.

THE SYNOD OF WHITBY

The argument was long and bitter. Agilbert (later to be Archbishop of Paris) asked Wilfred to represent him since he spoke the English language so much better. Agilbert was surely very fluent in Latin, but not so good in English, especially if it had a strong Northumbrian accent! It is interesting that the proceedings were not in Latin, the language of the Roman church.

King Oswy opened the proceedings, saying that all who served one God should observe the same rules and should not differ in celebrating the sacraments of Heaven. When the Synod had decided which was the truest tradition this must be loyally accepted by all.

Bishop Colman spoke first and defended the Easter practices of the Celtic church and especially of Iona, the home of their patron saint, Columba.

Wilfred replied and with withering scorn demolished Colman's arguments. The scene began to resemble the cut and thrust of a law court rather than a gathering of devout Christians humbly seeking the truth. All the rest of the world, said Wilfred, would accept the Roman way.

Colman said that he drew his authority from the disciple, St. John, but Wilfred put this aside saying Peter was the Prince of Apostles and Our Lord had said:

"Thou art Peter, and on this rock will I built my church ... and to thee will I give the keys of the kingdom of heaven."

Oswy asked Colman if this was true. (We must remember he could not read or write and did not possess the Gospels).

"It is true, your Majesty."

"Can you show that a similar authority was given to Columba?" asked Oswy.

"No," replied Colman truthfully.

"Then I tell you, Peter is guardian of the gates of Heaven and I shall not contradict him ... otherwise when I come to the gates he that holds the keys may not be willing to open them."

THE DECISION

Lady Hilda and her supporters had little option but to accept the ruling of the king and synod. Chad and Cedd also loyally accepted the decision.

Not so Colman. He and a large number of monks,— dissenters we might say, went back to Iona. From there he founded two monasteries, one of which was in the outer isles, where English and Scots fell out over the question of labour at harvest time,—some Scots expecting to eat having done no field work. The English then withdrew to a new monastery in Ireland, Mayo, where they flourished.

The implications of the decision of the Synod of Whitby were felt even by St. Cuthbert who, when he became Prior at Lindisfarne, was given a rough ride by some of the dissenting brothers (who had not retreated as far as Iona). With much tact and perseverance Cuthbert withdrew from their bickering and finally overcame the opposition.

670

In this year Oswy died aged 58,—probably the first Northumbrian king to die in his bed at what was considered a goodly age. He was succeeded by his second son, Egfrid.

For the greater part of his reign, Egfrid was at war, firstly with Mercia and its king Wulfera, then the Welsh and the Irish and finally the Scots. Is was they who lured him into an ambush in a narrow gorge and killed him and his men in 684.

During the last years of Lady Hilda's life, when she was building up the strength and reputation of her monastery while there was peace in Northumbria itself there were troubles in the church.

Wilfred, now Bishop of York, did not get on with King Egfrid. (Perhaps an old jealousy lingered from the days when Wilfred was a favourite of his brother, Alchfrid).

Egfrid was married for twelve years to Etheldreda, but she, a very devout lady, refused to consummate the marriage,— an act considered to be of great virtue by the church if not by her husband.

After begging the king that she might retire into a convent "at length she obtained his reluctant consent and entered the monastery of the Abbess Ebba (Egfrid's aunt) at Coldingham." In this act she had the full support of Wilfred. This incurred the king's great anger and his second wife seems to have hated Wilfred and had him expelled from York.

Wilfred was wealthy and powerful, but not powerful enough to oppose the king. He fled to the continent and appealed to the Pope.

Meanwhile Bosa, one of Hilda's monks, was appointed to York whilst Eata, abbot of Melrose, was offered Hexham. It looks as if Wilfred was not very popular in Northumbria, and perhaps insults at the Synod of Whitby were not easily forgotten.

When Wilfred returned in 680 waving the papal document confirming his right to Ripon and Hexham, King Egfrid had him arrested and imprisoned. He was then exiled to the south of England.

DEATH OF HILDA

680

In the same year Lady Hilda died. She had ruled her monastery as it grew in numbers and strength, upholding the ideals of poverty, chastity and simplicity in life as taught by the Celtic church.

Lady Hilda trained clergy, educated children and adults, sent out preachers and, perhaps most important of all, trained scribes to copy manuscripts and built up a famous library at Whitby.

Bede tells us that she was a woman of great energy and also one much beloved whom all called *Mother* because of her wonderful devotion and grace. This very probably is the origin of the term *Mother Superior* and she was perhaps the first to be so called.

She seems to have been forceful but not stubborn, giving way at the Synod when she felt it would be in the best interest of the Church. She was clearly not the type of super-efficient, thick-skinned woman we sometimes find in positions of authority today.

For the last six years of her life Lady Hilda suffered a long illness, most probably tuberculosis, with constant fevers.

Bede tells us:

She was attacked by a burning fever that racked her continually for six years; but during all this time she never ceased to give thanks to her Maker, or to instruct the flock committed to her both privately and publicly. For her own example taught them all to serve God rightly when in health, and to render thanks to him faithfully when in trouble or bodily weakness.

In the seventh year of her illness she suffered interior pains and her last day came. About dawn she received the holy viaticum and when she had summoned all the servants of Christ in the monastery, she urged them to maintain the gospel peace amongst themselves and with others. And while she was still speaking, she joyfully welcomed death and, in the words of our Lord, passed from death to life.

Lady Hilda died on the 17th of November 680. In the same year she had founded a new monastery at Hackness, about fourteen miles from Whitby.

One of the nuns there called Begu thought she heard the chapel bell sounding in the night and she saw the roof open and a great shining light. She saw Hilda's soul carried up to heaven by angels. Begu awoke and realised it was a vision. She roused the prioress, who called all the sisters into the church to pray for the soul of Hilda. At daybreak monks came from Whitby with news of Hilda's death. She was sixty-six.

HILDA'S RESTING PLACE.

It is thought that Lady Hilda was buried at Whitby, where King Edwin and King Oswy were also buried.

It may be that she rested at Hartlepool where in 1833 a saxon tombstone was found bearing the name HILDI-DRYTH (or THRYTH). The stone itself is displayed in St. Hilda's church at Hartlepool.

Bede does not actually say that she was buried at Whitby, but a twelfth century chronicle tells us that Edmund I, in 944 had the bones of St. Hilda together with some of those of St. Aidan from Lindisfarne and Ceolfrith from Wearmouth, taken to Glastonbury where he himself was to be buried. Perhaps that is where they are now.

Because of a belief in the literal resurrection of the body, the remains of saints were held to be of great importance to the faith. It was belived that on the day of judgment the saints would lead the faithful forward. Moreover, these 'holy bones' were believed to have miraculous powers in conferring healing and other blessings. Such relics were increasingly sought after and were purchased and even stolen or faked, (thus by the late middle ages St. Oswald had two heads—one in Durham and one in Luxemburg—three arms,—at Durham, Peterborough and Gloucester—and a complete body in Belgium).

WHITBY AFTER HILDA

Hilda was succeeded by her ward Aelfleda who had been dedicated to the monastic life by her father, King Oswy. After his death his wife, Eanfleda, also entered the monastery and became joint Abbess with her daughter. Aelfleda lived to the age of sixty, so she was abbess for thirty-six years.

Just over a century after Hilda's death the Viking raids on Northumbria began. Lindisfarne was pillaged and destroyed in 793. Whitby and the other coastal monasteries were probably attacked at this time. In 867 the Danes completed the work and the great abbey founded by St. Hilda was completely destroyed.

Or was it? For in 1078 re-building by the Normans began on an abbey which would dominate the landscape for more than five hundred years; built because St. Hilda was still known and revered three hundred years after her death. As we walk around the ruins let us remember:

Brothers, we are treading where the saints have trod.

LIFE IN THE ANGLO-SAXON MONASTERY
BUILDINGS

To picture the life in Lady Hilda's monastery the mind has to go back some thirteen hundred years. The first buildings to go up would be living and sleeping accommodation for the community, quickly followed by the most important building of all,—the church.

Probably the former were put up while the community were still living at Hartlepool, the workmen coming back and forth by boat. They would be made of timber with reed thatching as was the case at Lindisfarne. Then as stone gradually replaced the timber they would be built with dry stone walling technique, doubtless filling the cracks with lumps of clay. The art of making cement from ground limestone and sand had been lost with the departure of the Romans. At the begining of the next century Bede was intrigued to watch the makers of cement brought from the continent by the founder of Jarrow monastery, Benedict Biscop.

For the woodwork there were a variety of tools in use, axes, adzes, saws and even a lathe are described by Bede. Very soon there must have been finer tools developed for wood-carving and delicate work.

Some of the services would be held out of doors beside the great stone cross. At Hackness there are remains of one of these Crosses, showing very elaborate carving. Finer examples can be seen at Bewcastle and Ruthwell. The intricate designs worked on the stone shows what could be achieved with fairly primitive tools.

Dormitory buildings would eventually be replaced by separate cells to be used for prayer and study. During excavations at Whitby foundations of 7th century oblong buildings were found which could have been cells; they had space for a fire and a drain in one corner.

There was a common hall or refectory for meals and warmth, where a great fire would be lit in the centre of the room with only a smoke hole in the roof, so it was necessary to light the fire many hours before it was needed, to allow the smoke to clear. The fire was probably kept going all the time in order to avoid the need for re-lighting (with a flint and without paper) and excessive smoke. There was no shortage of wood, great areas were covered in forest although the moorland areas were even then much as they are today. (The moorland crosses tell us this, for these guide lines for the traveller would not have been visible in the midst of woodland).

In addition to the extensive workshops which surrounded the monastery there was also a separate house for the novices and a guest house (this must have been put to its fullest use at the Synod of Whitby). Probably even before these the school was built where pupils could be trained in Christian doctrine and Bible stories.

THE INFIRMARY

The infirmary was an important part of the monastery where caring for the sick and dying was regarded as a Christian duty. Sadly, it was generally the dying who went there as medical knowledge was almost non-existent. Later monasteries were to develop a great variety of herbal remedies, but not at this time.

Bede tells us of several plagues killing many monks and nuns, one example being at Jarrow when only one monk and one boy—thought to be Bede himself—survived. These plagues may have been typhus, cholera, diphtheria or even bubonic plague, carried by rats. With little hygeine and of course no soap or disinfectant, a whole community could be very quickly infected.

Even hot water in which to wash was a luxury. It is recorded of Etheldreda of Ely that she washed in hot water only before the greatest festivals, such as Easter and Epiphany, and even then only after she had "helped the other servants of Christ to wash."

It seems that it was generally the dying who were admitted to the infirmary and often their coffins were made ready and laid beside their bed. It was certainly a terminal hospital more concerned with the welfare of the soul than the body.

Whether the establishment that was at the present-day site of (hos) Spital Bridge was a hospice for visitors or a hospital in the infirmary sense is not clear. Certainly its foundation there was very ancient and in medieval times there was a leper hospital in that area. As far as that bridge is concerned it is recorded that there was a bridge over Spital Beck in the eleventh century. It is probable that the Anglo-Saxons would span the fairly wide beck with sturdy planks in order to reach their farmlands on the other side. There was no bridge over the Esk, just a ford between what is now Bog Hall and Spital Bridge.

ABBEY FARMS

In order to be self-sufficient the monastery had to have farms, raising stock and growing crops. It had to have extensive vegetable gardens and most probably a fishing community to supply the food.

Originally Caedmon was a cowherd working at one of the abbey farms. There would be many such workers as well as craftsmen, skilled in making things. There would be boat builders for much communication was by small coastal craft.

Bede tells us of a blacksmith whom he knew personally who "was much addicted to drunkenness, but the community bore with him patiently for they had need of his manual labour." So we can include among the necessary buildings a smithy and indeed, excavations revealed one at Whitby.

The Lady Hilda's type of monastic life was based on austerity and self-sufficiency, but not deprivation and self-abuse as practised by 'holy men' in the eastern hermitages and monasteries. The purpose of her foundation was twofold. Firstly, to provide a sanctuary where mass could be said daily, and men and women could give themselves to prayer for the salvation of souls. Secondly to provide facilities for learning and study and to make copies of the scriptures so that others might be taught.

To establish such a community and ensure its smooth running, Lady Hilda had to do a great deal of organising and administrative work. Her early experience in a fatherless female household would surely help her in this. She, of all people, well knew the capabilities of women in governing establishments.

FOOD

First of all, the community would have to be fed, the staple foods being meat, fish and bread. Wheat was widely grown in England and was one of the reasons why the Romans had come to Britain. Barley and oats also grew well in the northern climate. After harvest the corn would be threshed and ground, wholemeal naturally. Oatmeal would supplement this and also make porridge.

Though there was sufficient for these purposes, there was not enough grain to feed the stock. At the end of the autumn there was a great slaughtering of livestock,—some say this was the origin of Christmas-tide feasts. Meat was salted or smoked. (There was no lack of wood smoke from the fire in the great hall nor of salt from the sea). Fish could be given the same treatment. Perhaps the kipper is a very ancient sort of food!

As well as the domestic farm animals there was food for the catching in the wild life around the area; wild boar, deer, rabbits and hares as well as wild fowl could all be caught, so meat was seldom short. It was vegetables which were scarce in winter time. Peas and beans could be dried, but not the root vegetables, parsnips, turnips, onions and carrots.

Cauliflower and sprouts (and, need it be said? potatoes) are comparatively modern items, but cabbage was grown and in spring time young nettles, bistort leaves and wild garlic were gathered. Even seaweed was probably soaked and made into laverbread.

Basket-work beehives were everywhere, for honey was the only form of sweetening; the heather gave the bees nectar, as it does today. In summer time there were berries, apples and plums—smaller and more sour than we know today. There was milk from the goats and cows, thereby providing cheese which could be stored.

Imported spices were very precious, and necessary to disguise the taste of meat which was far from fresh. We know from one of Bede's pupils who wrote an account of the great

WINDSWEPT WEARMOUTH, site of Lady Hilda's first monastery, pictured as it was in the 18th century before the industrial revolution laid its grimy iron hand upon the landscape. (Reproduced by kind permission of Frank Graham).

WHITBY ABBEY. The remains of the Norman abbey, built three hundred years after St. Hilda's time, stand on the east cliff, probably on the same site as her monastery.

SPITAL BRIDGE. There has been a bridge here
since earliest times. This one was re-built in 1775, but
it is clear that the original stones have been re-used.
At one time this was the only road out of Whitby.
(When we developed this snapshot—taken with a
simple Brownie camera—we were surprised to see
the reflection under the bridge appear in the form of
a nun's face).

man's passing that he sent for "the few articles of value in my casket, so that I may distribute the gifts that God has given to me." They were: linen, incense and *pepper,* all of which were imported articles in short supply.

To drink, apart from water (several wells were sunk on the cliff) there was milk and,—for special occasions—mead, brewed from honey and barley. There was also a type of beer. Wine was used only occasionally for communion and it had to be imported, or at best transported from the south where a few vines were grown. Though Kent would have reasonable supplies, not very much would reach distant Whitby. Yet we hear of drunkenness. Bede refers to the destruction by fire of the monastery at Coldingham which he attributes to the sinful life of the inmates: "The cells which were built for prayer and study are now converted into places for eating, drinking, gossip or other amusements."

THE LIBRARY

Soon a school and a library would be added, each dependent on the other because books and manuscripts were very precious and rare. Manuscripts of the Gospels and the Psalms would be lent or bought by the enterprising and then they would be laboriously copied. They were, of course, written in Latin and this had to be learnt by the scholars who were not necessarily children, but grown men and woment. (An unnamed nun of Whitby wrote a life of Wilfred).

They had to learn long passages of the Bible by heart as their access to written books would be very limited. The scriptures were also taught in translation, so that the ordinary lay people could be told the Bible stories in their native tongue. It is said that Wifred knew all the Gospels by heart.

Scholars learnt to write on wax tablets on which the words could be erased over and over again. Several stylus pens for this purpose were found in the excavation at Whitby. Beeswax would be available for the tablets, but perhaps beginners were taught in wet sand.

Those pupils who showed most aptitude for it became scribes and copied the scriptures on to vellum. It was a painstaking and tedious job, especially in winter time. (An abbot of Jarrow writes a letter to accompany a book and apologises to the recipient that because of the severity of the weather "the hands of the scribes became sluggish and have not been able to copy a large number of books." We can imagine the frozen fingers and icy feet whilst standing in the stone-cold copying house (scriptorium). Another difficulty would be the light; there were lamps of a sort made by burning wicks in tallow; flaming torches would occasionally light the way outside and perhaps beeswax candles were used in the church.

As well as writing, there was also a whole system for calculating numbers up to ten thousand by positioning the fingers of one or both hands in different places on the body. The Arabic numerals we use were unknown in seventh century Europe. Since there is little evidence of coinage at this period it is probable that numbers were mainly used in counting flocks and chattels and calculating dates.

MANUSCRIPTS

The illuminated manuscripts, as in the Lindisfarne Gospels (now in the British Museum), were the work of special artists and craftsmen who used rare pigments of gold-leaf, blue lapiz-lazuli, purple from Mediterranean shell fish and red from north sea cockles. These and the inks were held in the tips of animal horns. Often only the first letter was illuminated but sometimes the whole page.

The script itself had to be very legible and uniform, so that it could be read all over Christendom. (Boniface as an old man asked that manuscripts sent to him should be clearly written and abbreviations and small letters avoided as his eyesight was not good).

Vellum was prepared in the monastery from calf-skin and parchment from sheepskin. More than a hundred animals, for example, would be needed to produce a psalter. A Northumbrian Bible, now in Florence, contains over two thousand pages of vellum and weighs around eighty pounds; each page measures about 28 by 20 inches. The handwriting indicates that there were as many as seven scholars working on it. It is small wonder that monks were required to learn the psalter, and often the Gospels too, by heart.

The books were the real treasures of the monasteries, for through them the thoughts of other ages could be carried to future generations.

The products of vellum clearly indicates that they also had tanneries and workmen skilled in leathercraft. They would produce boots and sandals, belts and harness for the animals and a wide variety of leather goods.

CLOTHING

Spinning and weaving of wool cloth went on in the monastery. In the excavations several spindle whorls and a fragment of woollen cloth were found.

There are many references to people being 'clothed' as monks or nuns, but we do not know what these special clothes were, nor how they could make a veil for nuns if they had only wool with which to work. Perhaps it was just the wimple around the face as later worn by medieval ladies.

Of the holy Etheldreda who founded the monastery at Ely (St. Audrey), it is said that from the time of her entry into the convent she never wore linen but only woollen garments. Was this the traditional hair shirt which tickled all the time so that mind had to prevail over matter? It also reveals the fact that linen was worn by upper class ladies and was probably imported from Ireland. (Linen needs ironing, so probably it was not too long until a flat-iron was made).

For winter wear, sheepskin jerkins and cloaks and leggings bound with crossed thongs would be used, for as we have said, leather work was a well known craft.

Small needles of bone and bronze were found at Whitby, but it is unlikely that knitting was known before the Vikings came, two hundred years later.

Some glass beads were found at Whitby, presumably to adorn someone, though perhaps not in Lady Hilda's day since glass manufacturers were brought from France only towards the end of her life. Before that the windows had no glass and had to be protected with wooden shutters.

WOOD

Wood was a very important raw material and, as we have noticed, there was an abundant supply and carpentry and carving were well advanced. Buckets for drawing well-water were made of it as were the water-tight barrels. This was a special skill, but not too difficult for experienced boat-builders.

There were trestle tables at which to eat and work, wooden forms and stools, probably wood bed bunks as the floor was very cold (and rats and mice not infrequent visitors). Wood bowls, spoons and plates were used, though there were bronze or silver utensils for the well-to-do.

THE COMMUNITY

In the twenty odd years of Lady Hilda's rule a thriving community was built up at Whitby. While not a commercial society, the standard of living was as high as anything then known in the country. It was the time of the Northumbrian golden age. What she had built up was a real family of men and women and even children.

There is mention in Bede of several very young children being in the care of the monasteries. Later, children under seven were not to be admitted, but from that age onwards boys would be accepted into the school and some trained for the choir.

Lady Hilda controlled people from all walks of life, for the monastery needed scholars and teachers, artisans and craftsmen in all the trades, women to do the weaving and sewing. Also, since the nuns did not go out to preach they probably did the bulk of the domestic work as well.

There were many farm labourers like Caedmon on all the abbey farms and general labourers for the building operations. There would be inshore fishermen and gardeners supplying much of the food for the growing community.

There must have been musicians, for the singing of the offices was very important and required training as there was no written music and probably only the harp to accompany singing.

THE RULE

Lady Hilda could decide what Rule of life should be followed in the monastery. She would be much influenced by Iona and Lindisfarne, but the Rule of St. Benedict was beginning to be well known (it was followed by Bishop Wilfred) and of increasing influence, tending to discourage the severity common in the Celtic church.

Extreme austerity was not encouraged by Lady Hilda, though fasting, abstemiousness and breaking sleep for the night office would be customary. The community was not shut away from the world, for secular visitors were many and frequent.

To organise and run such a place Lady Hilda would need all the ability and energy for which she was famous. If development could have continued to go forward from there, English history might have been very different, but invasion from Danes, Vikings and Normans were yet to come.

HACKNESS

This small "cell" was founded in 680, the year of Lady Hilda's death. She was almost certainly planning to spend the evening of her days in the sheltered seclusion of this remote place which lies several miles inland in a well watered woodland valley far away from the severe coastal winds. Even today the small village of Hackness holds a stillness and magic air of more remote times.

The ancient church there contains an interesting Saxon cross and the name Oedilburga carved thereon suggests that King Edwin's second wife, Ethelburga, who was grandmother to Lady Hilda's ward, Aelfleda, may have spent her retirement at Hackness. Since noble ladies married at a very early age— fifteen or thereabouts—Ethelburga was probably only a year or two older than Hilda. It is recorded that her daughter Eanfleda (widow of King Oswy) and her grand-daughter Aelfleda ruled jointly at Whitby after Lady Hilda's death.

The remains of the Saxon cross also depict the feet of some creatures which could well be geese and the scroll-like pattern at the base could also represent coiled snakes.

HOW DO WE KNOW?

There are great gaps in our knowledge of what went on in the seventh century A.D., but how do we know even as much as we do?

It is really a fascinating detective story with clues still being unearthed (and often in a very literal sense). All the clues available have then to be fitted together.

Firstly a great mental effort has to be made to project the mind into the life and ideas of that time. One must understand that to those converted to Christianity the Bible was a revealed way of life to be taken quite literally. The greatest stress was laid on the salvation of the soul, achieved by repentance for sins, prayer and good works. Illness, plagues, famine and distress were all accepted as God's will, often as a direct punishment for wrong-doing. It was an age of unquestioning faith.

ST. BEDE

About thirty years after Lady Hilda's death Bede, a monk at Jarrow, began to write his history of the church in England and this is the single great written source for telling us about the 7th and 8th centuries.

The monastery at Jarrow was even further developed than Whitby, with a wonderful library and much correspondence.

Bede lists the books he wrote,—more than fifty of them; short by our standards, perhaps, but not when we remember they were all written by hand on heavy parchment. Unfortunately very few have survived. Many were commentaries on books or passages of the Bible which were far from common knowledge in the seventh century.

Bede obtained his information from the monastery library and from hearing stories from other monks and sometimes from direct personal experience. He reports many miracles and visions—very often of the Hell awaiting unrepentant sinners— and sometimes heavenly premonitions and dreams; such things were a part of the accepted beliefs in his day.

*   *   *   *   *   *

There are a few other gleanings to be had from the near-contemporary manuscripts. There is an account of St. Bede's death at Jarrow and two Lives of St. Cuthbert who was, of course, Hilda's contemporary. Perhaps there are more manuscripts to be discovered on the continent or in the Vatican Library.

The chief way we can hope to find out is from archaeology. Objects unearthed can now be very accurately dated. Some of the Anglo-Saxon buildings in Whitby were uncovered in the 1925 excavations but they were filled in again after some artifacts had been removed. Such advances have been made since then that another 'dig' is needed now. Air photography is a great help in showing ancient boundaries, field systems and sites of buildings.

But, of course, *there is no money in it,* and the values of St. Hilda's and Bede's times have greatly changed. Few would deny that to most of us worldy goods, money and the pursuit of pleasure are our real driving forces. Yet the lives they led, the standards they valued, the buildings they constructed and the books they wrote have sent inspiring echoes ringing down the centuries

LEGENDS

Legends surround the saints. The two most well known about St. Hilda concern geese and snakes.

It was said that the wild geese stopped to rest at Whitby on their migratory flights to and from the Arctic. The majestic descent of these strange birds, coming from they knew not where, was easily ascribed to their paying homage to the well-loved Lady of Whitby. A later historian (Charlton) changed the geese into seagulls, since by this time the wide marshy estuary which attracted the weary wildfowl had been completely changed by man's reclamation.

As for the snakes, so firmly was it believed that the fossil ammonites found in the rocks below the abbey were originally these reptiles, that a snake's head is actually depicted emerging

from an ammonite on the town's coat of arms. It was but a short step to ascribe the presence of so many of these fossils to the miraculous powers of the Lady Hilda.

The Homily of St. Hilda

Trade with the gifts God has given you.

Bend your minds to holy learning that you may escape the fretting moth of littleness of mind that would wear out your souls.

Brace your wills to action that they may not be the spoils of weak desires.

Train your hearts and lips to song which gives courage to the soul.

Being buffeted by trials, learn to laugh.

Being reproved, give thanks.

Having failed, determine to succeed.

Whitby Abbey

The Abbey stands in a storm of snow
And rough waves rage on the rocks below
And many a season has come and gone
Since these old walls heard evensong
Since Caedmon stood in the stable stall
And heard the voice of the angel call,
And think now people of our town
Of the avenue of time gone down
Since Hilda prayed in this hallowed place
And lived her life of service and grace,
And think now people of our days
When Christian truth and Christian praise
Have spanned the years that have sped away,
Where do we stand in the world today?
For know ye now this simple fact
That no amount of human tact
Of human thought and human care
Can save us from a dread despair,
That only love in daily life
Redeems it from a fruitless strife.

17 November, 1980.   TOM STAMP.